The *Enchanting*
Christmas
COLORING BOOK

The Enchanting *Christmas*
COLORING BOOK

Beautiful Christmas scenes to color and complete

SIRIUS

SIRIUS

This edition published in 2017 by Sirius Publishing, a division of
Arcturus Publishing Limited,
26/27 Bickels Yard, 151–153 Bermondsey Street,
London SE1 3HA

ISBN: 978-1-78428-915-7
CH005698NT
Supplier 29, Date 0817, Print run 6303

Printed in China

Introduction

This coloring book brings Christmas to life through the wonderful drawings of Margaret Tarrant, a gifted illustrator of the early 20th century. From her depictions of children playing in the snow to contemplative winter landscapes and holiday decorations, the beauty of Christmas is revealed in all its aspects. Each line drawing is accompanied by the artist's original full-color illustrations which you can use as a guide or to set you off on your own path, as you prefer.

Margaret Tarrant was born in Battersea, a suburb of south London, on August 19, 1888, the only child of Sarah Wyatt and the painter and magazine illustrator Percy Tarrant, who encouraged her early artistic talents. As a child at home, Margaret would set up an "Exhibition Tent" with sheets, then pin up her artwork and invite her parents inside for a viewing. At school she often received prizes for her art. In 1905, she began to train as a teacher at Clapham School of Art, but her lack of confidence in her teaching ability meant that she didn't pursue this career. Instead her father helped his daughter to develop her professional drawing skills.

Tarrant was no stranger to depicting Christmas. At the age of eighteen, she began working for publishers of Christmas cards, where she perfected her unique romantic style.

Margaret honed her skills through many and varied commissions. Soon after the family's move to Gomshall, Surrey, she illustrated her first book, a new edition of Charles Kingsley's *The Water Babies* (1908). From this

point on, she applied her creativity and abilities as a figure artist to chronicling aspects of childhood, particularly imaginative play.

After becoming established as an illustrator, Margaret studied at Heatherley's School of Art in London, and then at Guilford School of Art. She also exhibited at the Royal Academy between 1914 and 1927, and at the Royal Birmingham Society of Artists.

In 1920, she began her most important business relationship, with the Medici Society. Named for the famous Italian family, the Medici Society was founded in 1908 to bring artists' work to the wider public. It began life with subscription-paying members before becoming a more traditional commercial enterprise.

A number of Margaret's paintings focused on spiritual subjects, including angels, and the Medici Society used them to illustrate a range of popular greeting cards and books. Her pictures of children adorned nurseries and school rooms throughout the

country. Some of these lovely images are included here for you to color in.

Her work for Medici ranged from books to posters and calendars and gave her wide exposure and huge popularity. It was in her professional life that she developed her two greatest friendships. The first was with Cicely Mary Barker, who she met while working on designs for a flower fairy alphabet. Both women adored children and held a deep love for the countryside. Both were popular artists known best for their fairies, and both displayed a sensitive approach to their subjects. The other great friendship Margaret developed was with Molly Brett, a colleague at the Medici Society who she met at Guilford School of Art in 1934.

Margaret worked in many media, including pen-and-ink, watercolor, and graphite. Though her approach was highly idealized, it was nonetheless grounded in close personal observation and she always drew from real life. According to a mother whose child Margaret had sketched, she would start various drawings as the child moved around, sketching an arm here, a leg there, returning to the sketch as the child resumed position again. She would then invent her composition, adapting the figures from the series of sketches. Margaret continued to work until 1953, when her health and eyesight began to fail her, six years before she died.

The magical images in the following pages provide a gateway into the open-hearted imagination of this talented artist. Margaret Tarrant's illustrations have been enjoyed by millions of people around the world. We hope their gentle and nostalgic beauty will lift your spirits as well.

Margaret W Torrent

Margaret W. Tarrant

Margaret W. Tarrant

Margaret W. Tarrant

Margaret W Tarrant

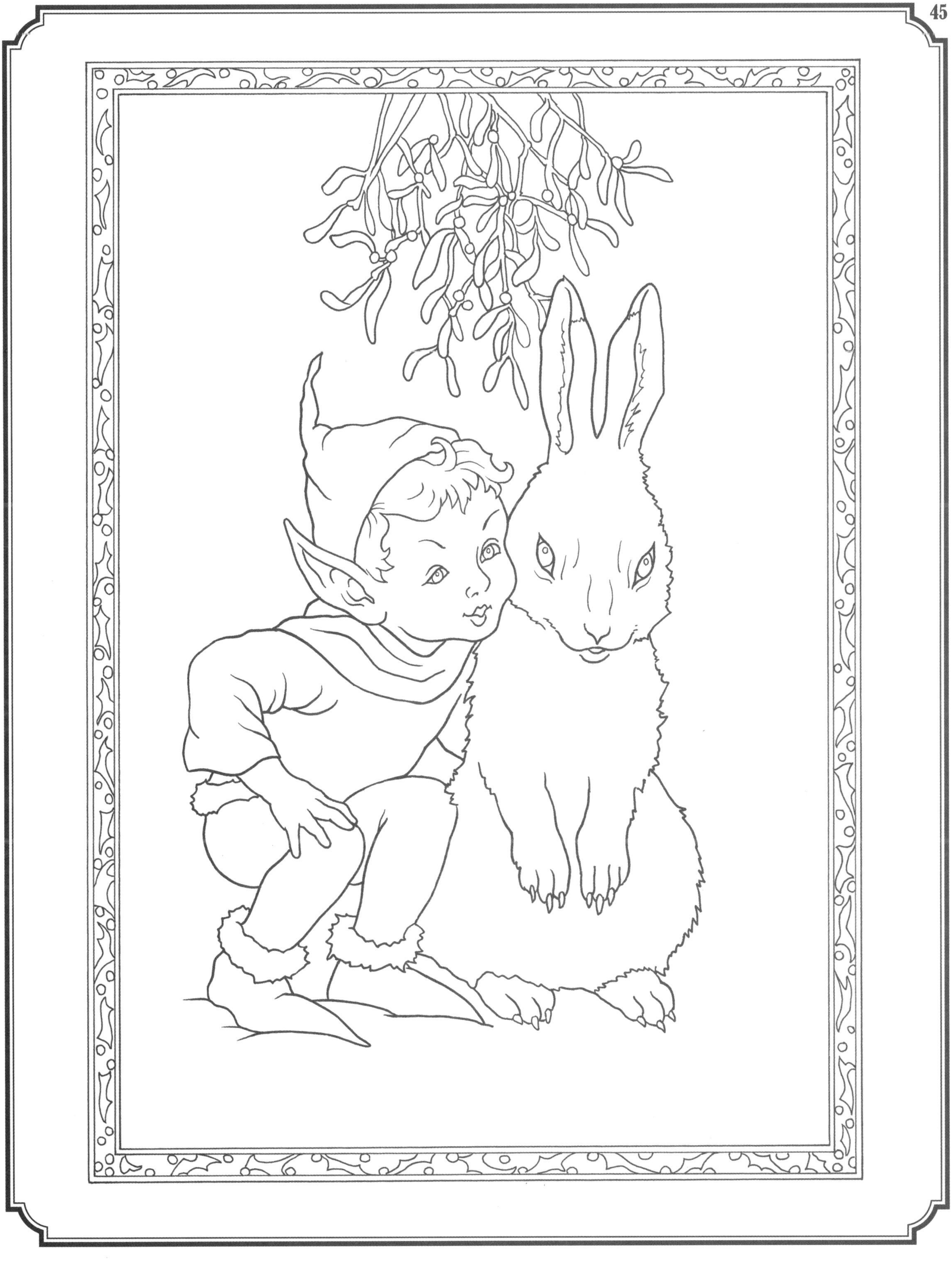

Margaret W. Tarrant

Margaret W. Tarrant

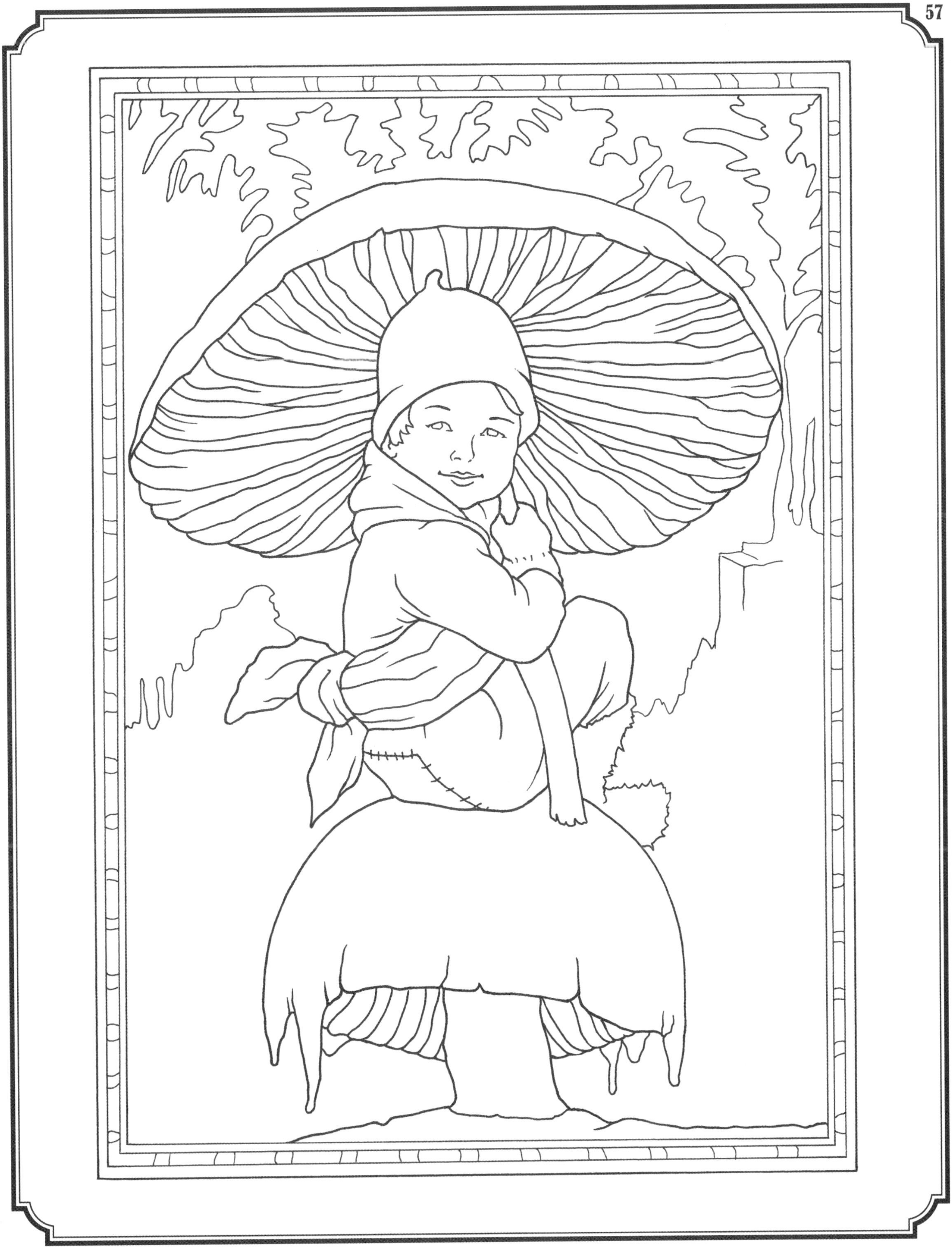

Margaret W. Tarrant

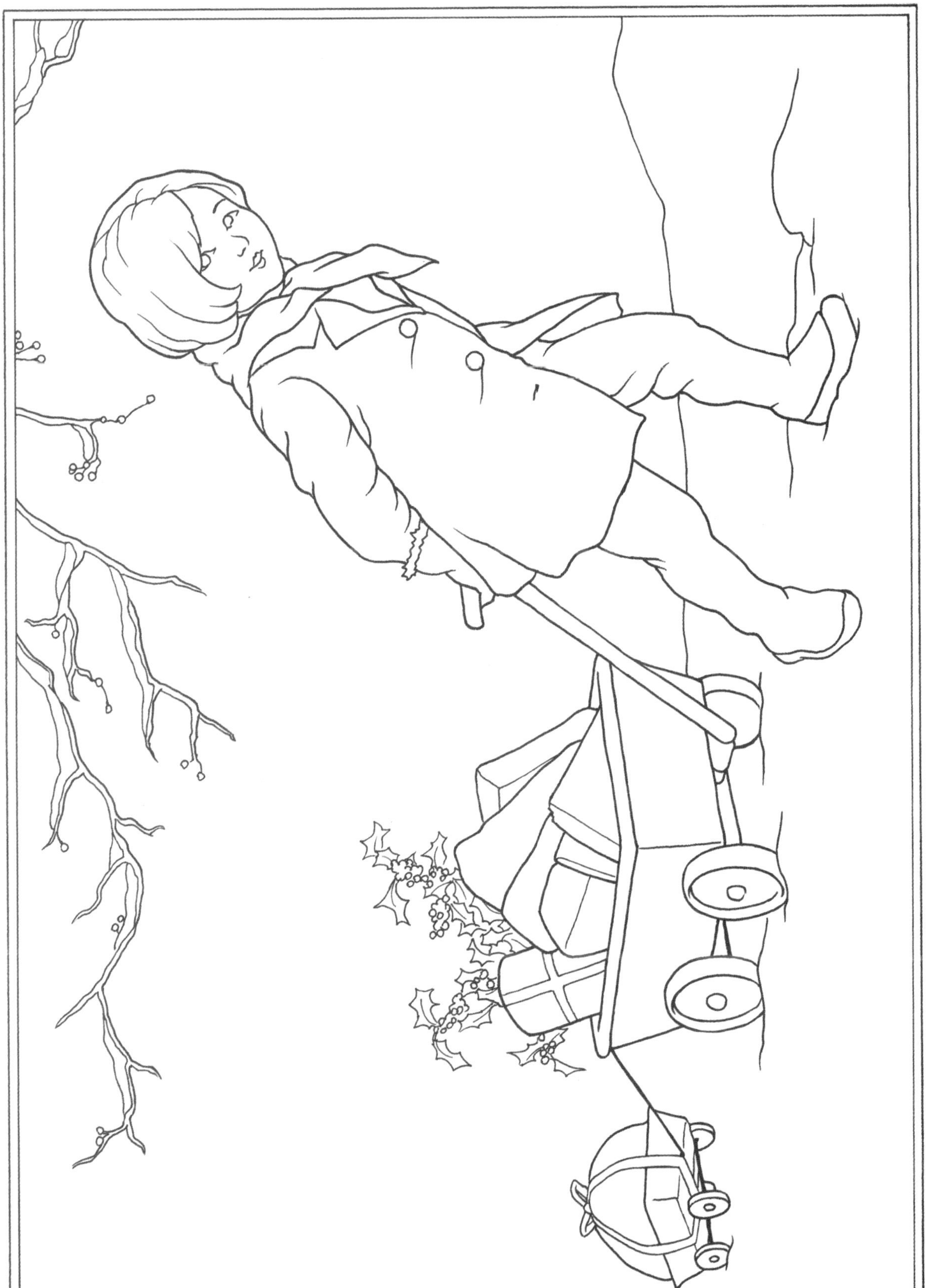

Margaret W Tarrant

Margaret W. Tarrant